
This book belongs to:

Made in United States
Orlando, FL
12 September 2023

36915111R00057